CLOWN AROUND

BY HELEN ORME
ILLUSTRATED BY SEB CAMAGAJEVAC

Titles in the Full Flight Thrills and Spills series:

The Knight Olympics	Jonny Zucker
Pied Piper of London	Danny Pearson
The Science Project	Jane A C West
Gorilla Thriller	Richard Taylor
Clone Zone	Jillian Powell
Clowning Around	Helen Orme
Time to go Home	David Orme
Haunted Car	Roger Hurn
Dinosaur Rampage	Craig Allen
Rubbish Ghost	Jillian Powell

Badger Publishing Limited
Oldmedow Road, Hardwick Industrial Estate,
King's Lynn PE30 4JJ
Telephone: 01438 791037

www.badgerlearning.co.uk

2 4 6 8 10 9 7 5 3

Clowning Around ISBN 978-1-84926-991-9

Text © Helen Orme 2013
Complete work © Badger Publishing Limited 2013
Second edition © 2014

All rights reserved. No part of this publication may be reproduced, stored in any form or by any means mechanical, electronic, recording or otherwise without the prior permission of the publisher.

The rights of Helen Orme to be identified as author of this Work has been asserted by her in accordance with the Copyright, Designs and Patents Act 1988.

Publisher: Susan Ross
Senior Editor: Danny Pearson
Designer: Fiona Grant
Illustrator: Seb Camagajevac

CLOWNING AROUND

Contents

CHAPTER 1	All the Fun of the Fair	5
CHAPTER 2	Out of this World	11
CHAPTER 3	All Aboard	15
CHAPTER 4	Fear Factor	19
CHAPTER 5	Who Are You Going to Call?	23

Clowns: Funny or Scary? 30

Questions about the Story 32

New words:

mascot

shrugged

shadowy

trapdoor

fairground

flickering

Main characters:

Cara

Jodie

Jamie-Lee

CHAPTER 1
All the Fun of the Fair

Cara picked up Jodie's clown doll and tried to stuff it in the cupboard.

"What are you doing to Mr Grin? Leave him alone!" said Jodie.

"I hate clowns, you know I do. They have creepy faces."

The three friends, Jodie, Cara and Jamie-Lee, were staying over at Jodie's house.

"But he's my lucky mascot," said Jodie, trying to grab the doll.

Cara swung the doll round by its leg and threw it into the corner of the room. Jamie-Lee tried to catch the doll, but couldn't.

She dropped her drink can. It bounced onto the floor.

"No!" Jodie screamed and leapt off the bed. "It's gone all over the mat. Mum will kill me!"

Jamie-Lee and Cara lay on the bed and giggled.

"Sorry," said Cara. "I didn't mean to."

"It doesn't matter whether you meant to or not," snapped Jodie. "Look at the mess."

Jamie-Lee leant over to look at the mat. The stain was dark purple and looked horribly sticky. She reached down to touch it and fell off the bed. That made Cara laugh even more.

"Come on," said Jodie. "Help me, we've got to get it clean or Mum will never let you stay over again."

Jamie-Lee mopped at the sticky mess with a piece of cloth she'd picked up off the floor.

"Hey! Get off! That's my best T-shirt." Cara leant over to grab it. She fell off the bed and banged her head.

By now, all three girls were on the floor of Jodie's new bedroom. She had only just moved house and it was the first time they had been allowed to stay.

Jodie's mum had gone to the shop so they were alone until she got back.

"If we get it clean quickly, your mum will never know," said Cara.

"Yeah, but how can we clean it?" Jodie was getting upset.

"Take it to the bathroom and dump it in the bath, then we can wash it off without making any more mess," said Jamie-Lee. She was always the one with good ideas.

"Roll it up," said Cara. "That'll make it easier to carry."

She started to roll it as she spoke.

"Hey look!" Jamie-Lee pointed to the floor.

"What is it?" asked Jodie.

"Not spiders," said Cara nervously. "I hate spiders."

"No, look! There's a door in the floor."

CHAPTER 2
Out of this World

"Did you know it was here?" asked Jamie-Lee.

"No, but then I've never tried to wash the mat before," said Jodie.

"How can you have a door in a floor?" asked Cara.

"It's a trapdoor," said Jamie-Lee. "They often had them in old houses so people could escape."

Jamie-Lee always knew the answers.

Sometimes it really annoyed the other two, but sometimes it could be useful.

"How old is your house?" asked Cara.

"Hundreds of years old," said Jodie. "That's why my parents bought it. They like really old things."

"Well, there you are then," said Jamie-Lee. "It leads to an escape tunnel."

"What would they want to escape from?" asked Cara.

"How should I know?" Jamie-Lee shrugged her shoulders. "I don't know everything."

Cara and Jodie looked at each other and smiled. At last, something she didn't know!

"Let's open it," suggested Cara.

"What about the mat?"

"We can do that in a minute. Come on Jodie – it's your bedroom – I think you should go first." Cara grabbed the handle of the trapdoor and started to pull.

"You'll never do it," said Jamie-Lee. "It will be stuck if it hasn't been used for hundreds of years."

But Jamie-Lee was wrong! The door lifted easily. Too easily.

The three girls bent over to look into the hole.

How it happened they never knew. Not one of them wanted to go down first. Somehow, somebody tripped and fell in and then they were all falling into the hole.

Chapter 3
All Aboard

Even before they could scream they found themselves outside in a field.

"How did we get here?" asked Jamie-Lee.

"Where are we?" asked Cara.

"It's the field next to our house," said Jodie. "Look, there's our back wall."

"How do we get back inside your house?" asked Cara. "Where did we come out?"

They looked all round but there was no sign of where they had come from.

"I don't like this, let's go back," said Jamie-Lee.

"Come on then, quick," said Cara. "If we go this way we'll get to that gate next to the house."

They started to follow Cara. The grass in the field was rough and it wasn't easy to walk through. It was getting dark and a thick mist was rising from the ground.

"Where are we now?" asked Jamie-Lee. "I can't see very well."

The mist was getting thicker and it was really hard to see where they were going.

Cara heard it first. "Listen," she said.

They all listened hard. The noise got louder and louder.

"It's a fairground, it's roundabout music," said Jamie-Lee.

"Let's go and see," said Cara.

As they moved towards the noise, they began to see lights and the shadowy shapes of tents and stalls.

Jodie looked back. She couldn't see her house now. There was nothing else to do. They had to go on. They had to get to the fair.

By this time they were all running. Jodie didn't know why she was running. She couldn't help herself. She hurried after Cara and Jamie-Lee. She didn't want to get left behind.

They were out of breath by the time they got to the fair. They stopped and looked round.

It was strange, very strange. Whatever was happening to them?

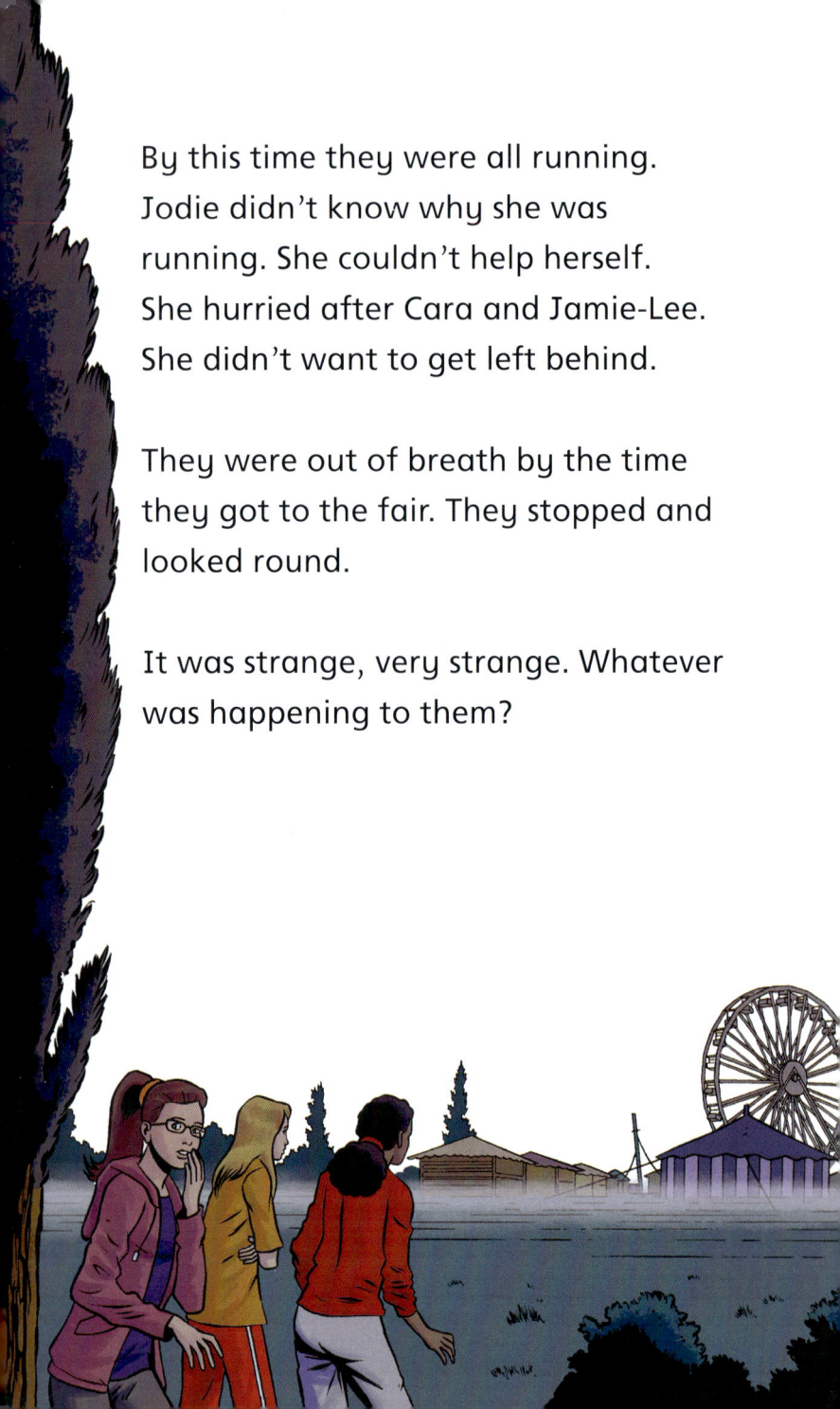

CHAPTER 4
Fear Factor

The music was still playing loudly and there were lights all around. But somehow the lights weren't right.

They seemed dim, not the bright, cheerful lights they had expected. And the music was the only sound. There were no voices. There were no people.

"I don't like this," said Cara.

"I want to go back," said Jamie-Lee. "Which way do we go?"

They both looked at Jodie.

"I don't know. I don't know where we are," she said.

Jodie looked towards the biggest tent. There was a flickering light inside. Suddenly, a flap was pushed back, letting more light shine out.

An arm appeared and waved to them. The three girls walked slowly towards the tent entrance. Jamie-Lee was the first to reach it. She went in.

Jodie and Cara followed quickly. As they stepped into the tent it suddenly went very cold.

Then, they saw them.

It was the most horrible thing Cara had ever seen in her life. Three large clowns, moving slowly towards them.

Cara wanted to run. She hated clowns anyway and this was just too creepy, but she couldn't move. Jamie-Lee reached out a hand and grabbed Cara. Jodie moved closer to them both.

As the girls moved together, the clowns reached them. They were huge.

They opened their mouths as if they were going to speak. But there was no sound.

Cara tried to say something, but no words came out.

The clowns stood and looked at the girls. Cara wanted to look away, but she couldn't even close her eyes. The clowns got closer and closer.

They were horrible. They had painted grins on their faces. They each had one black eye and one blue eye. Their eyes were fixed on the girls and held them totally still.

Jodie was terrified. What was going to happen to them? However would they escape?

CHAPTER 5

Who Are You Going to Call?

Cara tried to look away. Out of the corner of her eye she saw another light coming closer. A flickering candle light. Whatever was it now? What else could be coming for them?

The clowns didn't move. They just stood in front of the girls. Looking and grinning.

The candle light got brighter and closer.

Jodie and Jamie-Lee tried to look away from the clowns' faces, but they couldn't. They couldn't move at all.

Then Cara saw who was carrying the candle. She gasped. Moving towards them was Jodie's toy clown.

But it had grown. It was just as big as the ones in front of them. Now she was really scared.

The toy clown got closer. It reached the group and held out the candle towards the nearest clown, the one staring at Jodie.

The clown turned to look at the toy. As it did so, the candle moved closer to its face. And its face began to melt.

The smile was pulled downwards. The blue eye blurred and fell out of its face. Its whole face turned into melting wax and poured down to form a big puddle on the floor. The clown collapsed gently down into the puddle. Suddenly, Jodie was free. She could move again.

Jodie's toy turned to the next clown and the same thing happened. Now Cara could move too. Then it was Jamie-Lee's turn to be freed.

The girls looked at each other. Jodie looked at her toy.

"Take us home – please," she whispered.

The toy moved towards them. What now? Was it going to help? Or had things just got worse?

Cara groaned and sat up.

Jodie shook Cara gently.

"You just bumped your head. Are you OK? " asked Jamie-Lee.

"I've just had the most horrible dream," said Cara.

"Come on," said Jodie. "I've got to do something about this mess before mum gets home."

Jamie-Lee looked at her. "What was your dream about?"

Cara pulled a face. "About clowns," she said.

Then they heard the door open and shut downstairs.

"I'm home," called Jodie's mum.

"Quick," said Jodie. She picked up the mat and dragged it out to the bathroom. The others followed.

Underneath, the wooden floorboards were clean, polished and solid.

There was no trapdoor.

The bedroom door closed with a bang behind them. Jodie's clown doll sat up on the bed and grinned. It looked towards the mirror. The faces of the clowns with one black eye and one blue eye glared back out at him.

Slowly the clown doll closed one eye and winked.

Clowns: Funny or Scary?

Most people love clowns as a form of entertainment, but just a few think that clowns are really scary. When someone is very scared of something it is called a phobia.

Clown phobia is known as **coulrophobia.**

Why do some people think clowns are scary?

It may be because a clown's face is covered with make-up. Some people say that you cannot tell whether a clown is friendly or not when you look at its face.

When were the first clowns?

The first records of clowns go back thousands of years. There were clowns in the time of the Ancient Egyptians (around 5000 years ago).

How do you recognise a clown?

Clowns have heavily made-up faces. Often they have a white face. They paint on huge lips and big eyes. Sometimes they have a big, red nose.

What do clowns wear?

Clowns often wear brightly coloured wigs and colourful coats. They may have very baggy trousers and often wear oversized shoes.

How do you get to be a clown?

Clowns need to be physically fit. They have to learn to fall over without hurting themselves. There are even clown schools where people can go to learn everything they need to know. They teach skills such as miming, juggling, acrobatics and magic tricks.

Questions about the Story

What was Jamie-Lee's explanation for the door in the floor?

Is it likely that there would be a trapdoor that no one had noticed?

What was strange about the place where they ended up after falling down the hole?

Why wasn't the fair what they had expected?

Why were the three large clowns so creepy?

At the beginning of the story, Cara bangs her head, but this isn't mentioned again until the end of the story. What does this make you think about Cara's dream?

When they moved the mat at the end of the story, there was no trapdoor. Why didn't any of the girls comment on this?